# GOD'S HAND UPON ME

## Memoirs of Emilie Ballard, Book I

"You had my mother give birth to me. You made me trust you while I was still a baby. I have leaned on you since the day I was born; you have been my God since my mother gave me birth."

Psalm 22: 9-10, EV

authorHOUSE®

AuthorHouse™
1663 Liberty Drive
Bloomington, IN 47403
www.authorhouse.com
Phone: 1-800-839-8640

Published by AuthorHouse  12/08/2014

ISBN: 978-1-4969-4883-0 (sc)
ISBN: 978-1-4969-4882-3 (e)

Library of Congress Control Number: 2014918863

# Preface

God has blessed me richly throughout my long life. For some years I have thought that eventually I would write up my memoirs. That is why I saved all letters, manuscripts, and photos that might be useful when the time finally came to do so. I envision three or four volumes. Book I would be about my family background, and my life and experiences during my first thirty-nine years of life. It would end with my appointment as a missionary to work with the Karen people of Burma. Book II would be about my work and experiences in Burma, now called Myanmar. Book III would be about my work and experiences in Thailand. I'm not sure whether my experiences since retirement should be part of Book III or should be Book IV. Of course, much depends on whether God chooses to let me live long enough to complete all of these or not.

I owe a great deal of gratitude to those who have made this first book possible. First, I thank Maggie Hover for proofreading my manuscript. She made a number of suggestions so that it would be easier for the younger generation to understand. Then I am deeply grateful to the many Karen people now living here who have donated funds to pay for publishing this volume. I am grateful to my father for saving all of my letters to him from childhood on. I am also very grateful to my good friend, Samantha Foster. She helped me with using the computer and printer. Without her help, I wouldn't have been able to get the book written.

I made notes from the materials I had and scanned the photos I wanted to save. Then I sent most of the original materials to my sister's daughter, Phyllis Sorrell. She lives in Las Cruces, NM, and has become interested in the family genealogy. However, as for photos of my brother, only sent copies to her. The originals were sent to his adopted son, Robin Ballard in San Diego, CA.

# Family Background and Early Childhood

By God's grace I was born into a Christian home. My parents were actively engaged in the ministries of an active mission-minded church. As a result, I can't remember a time when I didn't believe in God and His Son Jesus Christ.

My mother, Gertrude Emerson Long, was born in Maine and later the family moved to Massachusetts. Her father, Joseph Mansfield Long, was a minister. Mother was the fourth of his seven children. However, after his wife, my Grandmother Ida Carroll Snell Long, had her last child, she began having mental and emotional problems. Because of that, Grandfather moved with his whole family to Washington, DC. They settled in the area known as Brookland in northeast Washington. There he got a job with the civil service.

My father, Walter Raymond Ballard, was born in Illinois, but later the family moved to Kansas. I no longer remember the names of his parents. He was the oldest of three children. He graduated from the agricultural college in Manchester, Kansas, in 1905. For six months he was connected with the Kansas City Park Board. Then he came to the University of Maryland Experiment Station. There he specialized to a considerable extent with plant breeding of fruits. In September 1918, he married the one who became my mother. They settled down in a small house with a large yard in Hyattsville, Maryland, just two and a half miles from the University. He was then twenty-eight years old and she was eighteen. I was born the following year on July twenty-first. I was named after my mother's favorite high school teacher, Miss Emilie Margaret White.

The First Baptist Church of Hyattsville was just four blocks from our house and my parents soon became active in its ministries. The church was dually aligned with both the American Baptist Convention and the Southern Baptist Convention. However, it used the literature and organizational structure of the Southern Baptists. From the time I could be carried to church I was enrolled in the Cradle Roll Department. Over the years, I progressed to Nursery, Kindergarten, Primary, and Junior departments. The church also had a strong missions department.. Thus, when I was in the Primary Department, I was also enrolled in the Sunbeams. While I was a Junior, I was active in the Girls Auxiliary. Boys were enrolled in the Royal Ambassadors. In both organizations we learned about boys and girls in other countries. We were taught about their culture, their need of Jesus, and the work of the missionaries. The church was a member of the District of Columbia Convention, which was also dually aligned. Because of that, we often had missionary speakers from the two conventions. From the age of seven I began saying that I wanted to be a missionary when I grew up.

In the meantime two more children had been added to our family. My sister, Dorothy Isabel, was two and a half years younger than I. At the time she was born, we had two aunts named Dorothy. That is why we took the first three letters of her first name and the first two letters of her second name and called her Doris. She was a beautiful little girl. Whenever people saw her they exclaimed over her but ignored me altogether as though I were invisible. I don't think that I resented my sister's beauty so much as I resented people's ignoring me. However, there were so many things that I was interested in that I simply didn't try to compete with her. I could see that it would be futile anyway.. In fact, I never had any interest in trying to beautify myself. She and I were opposites to each other not only in temperament, but also in aptitudes. It was no secret that I was Daddy's favorite and she was Mother's favorite, but both parents strove to treat both of us the same. I am grateful for that.

My brother, Arthur Holcomb, was six years younger than I and he looked a great deal like my father. He had curly hair whereas we girls had straight hair, which didn't seem fair to us girls. Only when he was two years old did his hair get cut the first time. At that time both of us girls had fairly long hair. On the day that his hair was to be cut, all three of us were taken to a photographer's shop. We had our picture taken there. Then all three of us were taken to get our hair cut short. Again we had our picture taken. It was amazing how much older the short hair made us look.

As far as I know, we had a normal life growing up. During the Depression years we children weren't aware of the economic situation at all. We always had good, nourishing meals. I don't remember whether Mother made any of our clothes or not. Once a year we would go on the trolley car into Washington to buy a new Easter outfit. We had the usual childhood diseases like measles, mumps, whooping cough, chicken pox. I don't recall any other serious diseases or injuries. We played together with other children in the neighborhood. Often at night after the supper dishes were cleaned up Daddy would read stories to us.

I particularly remember his reading us the Uncle Remus stories. He was very good at imitating the southern drawl of Uncle Remus. The stories were about animals and their adventures and escapades. One of the main characters was Br'er Rabbit. He seemed to be smarter than the other animals and always managed to get out of scrapes.

Since my mother's family all lived close by, we saw each other often. As mentioned above, Grandmother developed post-partum depression after the birth of her seventh child. In those days mental disorders were an embarrassment which nobody talked about. Many times we were not taken to visit her, being told that she was not well. But at other times she was okay and was happy for us to see her. Because of her illness, Grandfather left the pastorate and moved with his family to 'Washington, DC.

Mother's oldest sibling was named Dorothy Mansfield Long. When I was learning to talk, I tried to call her name and it came out "Duffy". From then on she was always Duffy to us children. She never married but became a lawyer. The next of Mother's siblings was Hallock Porter Long. He also became a lawyer along with Mother's younger brother Carleton. These three siblings set up their own law practice to handle civil cases. Hallock remained a bachelor until he was around fifty years old. Then he married a woman named Pauline. Carleton married Dorothy Fisher and they had one daughter named Margaret. Mother's third sibling, George, was killed while in military service during World War I.

Mother's younger sister was named Katherine Edward Long, but she was always "Katz" to us children. She was married to a widower named Bernard Bartoo who had four sons. It was an arranged marriage. The oldest son was her age when she married Bernard. Mother's youngest sibling was named Bryant Alden Long and he was just eight years older than I. He worked for a number of years in the Railway Mail Service. His wife was named Dorothy Jane. They had two sons, Alden and Gene. One day he tripped over something while sorting mail on the moving train. After hospitalization he went onto disability This made him very unhappy and he soon developed depression.

Mother's family is a direct descendant of John and Priscilla Alden. They were part of the first settlers from England to America and were called Pilgrims. In later years Hallock did a lot of research on the family genealogy. I believe two booklets are in the Library of Congress in Washington, DC. One traces his father's line, the Longs, and the other his mother's line, the Snells.


Daddy's extended family all lived either in Kansas or Oklahoma. We only visited them once while we were children. I was just seven, Doris was five, and Arthur was one year old. We traveled by train in two compartments across the aisle from each other. My brother was put into the cover of a suitcase during the trip in order to not roll around. After we arrived at Daddy's sister's home, he was put to bed in a bureau drawer. Daddy's sister, Gertrude Ballard Mitchelson, and her husband, Roy Mitchelson, had eight children. Daddy's youngest sibling was named Arthur. I no longer remember what Daddy's parents' names were. The family lived in Baxter Springs, Kansas.

We didn't see them again until we were grown. However, we were kept informed about them by what was called the Ballard Round Robin Letters. A regular circuit was set up among all members of the extended family. When the letters reached one of the members, that person would remove his/her previous letter. Then an update on the person's family news would be inserted. Sometimes comments on news in the letters from other members were also included. Then it would be sent on to the next person on the circuit, who would do as the first one had done. The letters usually took about four months to make the rounds.

At one point Daddy learned from the Round Robin Letters that two fourth generation cousins of his had moved to Washington. One was named Russell Wooden and the other Sallie Vest. Neither of them had married. Daddy got in touch with them and invited them to our house for a meal. After that, they were regular guests at our Thanksgiving and Christmas dinners until Mother's death. In later years Russell researched and wrote up the genealogy of our branch of the Ballard family. He called it Ballardina. He sent mimeographed copies to everyone on the Round Robin circuit. Many of the recipients sent updates and/or corrections. Then he made a revision and again sent mimeographed copies to everyone on the circuit.

I started school the fall that I was six years old and really enjoyed it. I took to reading like a duck takes to water. My first grade teacher told Daddy I had learned to read amazingly fast. I guess my aptitude for languages was showing up already. The teacher told Daddy that I would bring home a new reader and read it through from beginning to end by the next day. Each classroom had a library from which we could borrow books for a few days at a time. While I was in the second grade, I read not only all of the books in the second grade library but all of those in the third grade library as well. When I was in the third grade, Daddy got me a library card for the local public library. Then I could borrow three or four books at a time for two weeks. Daddy also bought books for us. I especially remember the Book House series. My favorite was the volume on stories of knights and their adventures. I also devoured the Bible Story books he gave me. Often in the afternoon I would get a book and lie down behind the furniture in the living room. There I wouldn't be seen and I could read and read. Of course, the light was not very good. It no doubt was harmful to my eyes, but I managed somehow.

We owned four good-sized lots. Our house was on one lot. The lot beside it made a good side yard for us kids to play in. The two back lots were about ten feet below the front two. That was where Daddy had his garden, which was his hobby. He mostly planted flowers as he was experimenting with cross-breeding bulbous plants. He also grew gooseberries and currants and had a peach tree, a pear tree, a crabapple tree, an apple tree, and a cherry tree. I especially remember helping my mother prepare and can cherries in quart bottles in a pressure cooker. We had a cellar under our house which was always damp and cool. Daddy put shelves down there on which to store food my mother had canned. In that way we always had some fruit and vegetables to eat in the winter months.

Daddy was an extension agent in the University of Maryland's agricultural department. Sometimes in the fall Daddy would go away for a month at a time in connection with his work. Each year on one of those trips he brought back a bushel basket each of several kinds of apples. These he also stored in the cellar so that they would keep well. He travelled with a home demonstration worker. Among other things, they went to the various county fairs to help judge plants, animals, and produce. The farm women brought baked goods to be judged also. Daddy said that one of the most enjoyable aspects of his job was sampling each entry.

I was quite a tomboy. I often said that I was glad I was born a girl. If girls were called tomboys, it wasn't anything to be ashamed of. On the other hand, if boys were called sissies, that was a slur. We had a maple tree at the corner of the yard in front of the house. It divided into two trunks about four feet above the ground. I loved to climb that tree. We rarely went to the movies because the church frowned on such activity. However, once my mother took me to see the children's movie, Tarzan. I was really fascinated with the way that he could swing from branch to branch. After I got home, I tried to imitate him in the maple tree. Of course, there were no vines to swing on. Still, I got so I could drop from limb to limb to get from the top to the bottom in a very short time. One day I was high up in the tree when a big storm was coming. Soon a strong wind began to blow the branches back and forth quite hard. It was exhilarating to me. I gave myself to it to let the wind take me along with the branches wherever it would. Of course, Mother was worried that lightning might strike. She demanded that I come down immediately. After a few more minutes, I reluctantly came on down.

The boy who lived next door was lent a two-wheeled bicycle for a day. While he was at lunch, he let me use it. The street had a gentle slope from his house down past ours. During the hour that I had the bike, I got so that I could coast down the slope all the way without having to put my foot on the ground. Then, when he came out to get the bicycle, I wanted to show him what I could do. This time, I ended up in a rosebush. That was the only time I ever rode a bicycle. My folks didn't dare get me one. They said I'd go off and kill myself the first thing. That's how rambunctious I was.

During the last month before the end of my fourth grade something unusual happened. All school children were given an eye exam. When it was my turn, I had to walk up to eight feet from the eye chart in order to make out the largest letter on the chart. In those days it hadn't occurred to most people that children might need glasses. Consequently, the teachers were all amazed at my poor eyesight. Yet I was not a behavior problem, so I was always assigned to a seat in the back of the room. Then I always had to go clear up front in order to copy anything off of the front blackboard.

Another girl and I both came to school the last day wearing eyeglasses. She cried the whole morning because she felt so conspicuous. The next year she came to school without glasses, so evidently her eyesight wasn't that poor. As for me, the glasses made all the difference in the world! I was really glad to have them. Before, the leaves on the trees above my head were fuzzy. The lighted street lights at night had many concentric rings of colored light around them. The glasses brought everything into sharp focus.

Once all of us children were in school, Mother began teaching piano to children who came to our house for the lessons. She began to teach me also. Because she was also involved in many other activities, she often postponed my lessons. As a result it took me a year to get through Book One.

9

In the sixth grade among other things we learned about the Spartans of Greece. They toughened themselves up by not wearing extra clothes over their tunics even in the coldest weather. Somehow, this appealed to me, and I wanted to toughen myself up the same way. Of course, Mother wouldn't let me leave the house without wearing my warm coat in the winter. I would go by way of a back alley not far from home. Then I would take off my coat, and hide it under the overhanging bushes. After that I would continue on to school without it. Finally it got cold enough that my arms were covered with goose pimples. Then I condescended to wear a sweater so that people wouldn't see the goose pimples. People seeing me on the way to school felt sorry for me. One day a woman came out of her house with a coat for me to wear, which I refused. Of course, I didn't dare tell anyone why I was doing this. I knew that they wouldn't appreciate my reasoning. When I returned home at the end of the day, I would go through the alley. There I retrieved my winter coat and wore it to the house.

I succeeded in proving to myself that I could do it. I didn't even catch a cold during that time. However, the next year I didn't know how to start wearing a coat like other people. I was afraid that people would ask me why I had done without it the year before. I didn't want to reveal my reason. Fortunately,, that year I became a strong admirer of a girl in the church who was four years older than I. After a few weeks of going without my coat, she confronted me. She said that if I didn't start wearing a coat, she wouldn't speak to me anymore. That gave me a reason that I could tell people, and so I was saved from my dilemma.

My mother's youngest brother, Bryant, usually came along with Grandfather to our house on Sundays after the morning service. They stayed for the noon meal and throughout the afternoon. After dinner Mother did the dishes and cleaned up the kitchen. Then she would come and play hymns on the piano in the living room. Grandfather also brought out one of his horns or stringed instruments, for he had many kinds. The rest of us would sing along. This would continue for an hour or more and was most enjoyable. In the evening we went to the Baptist Young People's Union, which started at seven p.m. It was a training union, usually abbreviated BYPU. The adults also had a meeting at that time.

The training union for children and young people was where we were trained to become leaders. We learned to pray out loud, read Scripture, sing solos or duets, tell a short printed message in our own words, and lead meetings. When I was about eleven years old, the BYPU of the DC Convention sponsored a Bible memorization contest. Each church had its own local contest first to choose its representative. There was a list of a dozen or more chapters of the Bible from which we could choose. I decided that I wanted to enter, and chose the longest of all the passages, which was Matthew 5. However, Mother thought that some parts of it were not appropriate for children, so I memorized Matthew 6 instead. I recited it all correctly during the contest. However, a girl in her teens used more expression in her recitation and she was chosen as the winner.

During Sunday afternoons following the hymn sing, we children were allowed to play quietly while the adults rested. Bryant would often tell stories to us three children. At one time he started a series story which he evidently made up week by week, called Threadwhiskers. It was about the adventures of a kitten which got its whiskers burnt off because it was naughty and didn't obey its mother. Its mother then glued some threads on where the whiskers had been. From then on he was the butt of teasing from other kittens and was nicknamed Threadwhiskers. He had heard that the King of the Cats, who was a Persian cat, of course, could give him back real whiskers. He had many adventures as he tried to find his way to the King. The only thing I remember is that he once rode somewhere on a trolley car. He paid his fare with cheese. The conductor was a cat and with cheese as bait he could catch mice to eat.

Another pastime that Bryant got me engaged in was creating a "Bug City". We placed stones and pieces of brick as houses in orderly rows with a number of "streets" to form a "city". Then each Sunday we would lift up the stones one by one to see what "tenants" had moved in.

My father, having majored in entymology in college, then got me interested in raising caterpillars. We watched them spin their cocoons. We also discovered which kind of moth or butterfly each one turned into. We set a small glass partly filled with water into a fish bowl. We placed twigs of leaves for the caterpillars into the glass. Then we covered the fish bowl with cheesecloth held in place by a string tied around the outside neck of the bowl. Mother was a bit squeamish about our doing this. However, none of the caterpillars ever got away.

Daddy also got me interested in making an insect collection. He showed me how to put the insects into a cyanide bottle to asphyxiate them. Then on the nest day we mounted them on pins in a special box for the purpose. With such experiences I soon learned the difference between a bug and a beetle and between a moth and a butterfly. Thus, I learned to have somewhat of an interest in insects and not be squeamish in handling them.

It was our custom to spend two weeks at the beach each summer. We travelled by trolley car, transferring in Washington to another line ending at Glen Echo. Here there was an amusement park on the shore of the Chesapeake Bay at what was called North Beach. Daddy would go with us and stay overnight. Then he returned home to work in his garden. This was a more enjoyable vacation for him than the beach. The day before our two weeks was up, he returned and spent one night with us again. Then he escorted us back home once more. The water in the Bay never got very deep in the summer. Thus, it seemed a safe place for us children to play in the water while Mother watched us from the shore. Sometimes she joined us in the water.

Of course, we didn't stay in the water all the time. We stayed in a hotel of sorts. Each person or family had a private room for sleeping and having private family times together. However, I seem to think that we spent a lot of time down in the big main room, eating together and visiting with each other. There was an African American servant woman who had a daughter about my age . We were allowed to play with her since my mother could see that the child was obedient and thoughtful.

One day as my mother entered the main room from outside, her heel caught on something and she started to fall. In an effort to catch herself she ran across the room half falling. When she reached the opposite wall, she caught the wall with her outstretched arm. The impact dislocated her shoulder and the pain was excruciating. Soon, a doctor arrived. He got several persons there to hold onto my mother's body. At the same time, he pulled her arm enough to get it back into the socket. She mostly kept her arm in a sling for several weeks after that because of the swelling and soreness of her shoulder. Yet the hurting was nothing like the severe pain when the shoulder had been dislocated.

In 1930 Mother joined a tour group to go and see the Passion Play in Oberamagau, Germany. The tour took them through England, Belgium, Holland, and Germany. My father hired a woman to live with us during Mother's trip. She took care of the home and us children and prepared meals for all of us. Her name, Coita Edrington, was so unusual that I still remember it.

I was old enough that it was my job to mow the side lawn every Saturday. One week my five-year-old brother started picking up little twigs and dropping them onto the lawnmower's blades as they turned. It was fun to see the blades chop them up. However, one time he got his fingers too close to the blades. A tiny bit of the end of his thumb was cut off. Of course, he began to scream! Coita came running out of the house and hurried him into the bathroom. She quickly turned on the tub faucet and held his thumb under it. All of a sudden his screaming stopped and there was silence. We were mystified, but it turned out that somehow he thought that his whole thumb would have to be amputated. Once Coita realized that, she assured him that he wouldn't lose his thumb. Immediately, he stopped screaming and didn't even whimper any more.

When Mother got back home, she showed us a number of interesting artifacts, picture postcards, and photos. She loved the castles along the Rhine River in Germany. She was especially impressed that in Holland the women even had clean lace curtains in the cow barns. Of course, she thought the Passion Play was fabulous! It made Christ's passion seem very real to her.

I think it was when I was eleven years old that I became restless in Sunday School. I was already familiar with most of the Bible stories that were being taught. Whenever the teacher asked questions, I quickly answered them not giving the other children a chance to answer. In the meantime I annoyed the children, pinching them or sticking them with straight pins. During the opening assembly of the Sunday School, I started sticking the teacher sitting in front of me with a straight pin. She would jump a little and squirm a little. Of course, she was supposed to set an example for the children. That is why she didn't dare scold me during the assembly. Then I made it a point to leave for my classroom as soon as the assembly was over. I must have been a real trial to the teachers!

In the summer of that year my Sunday School teacher asked me whether I had thought about being baptized. I knew that I believed in Jesus and that He died to pay for my sins. Now her question made me realize that I needed to publicly take a stand for Christ. When I asked permission from my father, he replied that he thought I was still too young. The next year the teacher asked me again, and this time my father gave permission. I was baptized on August 15, 1931 and I really did want to live the way that would please the Lord.

# My Teenage Years

When I became a teenager a whole new life opened up to me. I had new experiences and opportunities. I also had new energy and interest to enjoy and learn from them. In the first place I entered high school. The Hyattsville High School was a mile away from home. In those days few people had cars and almost everybody walked everywhere. I walked to school regularly with my load of books in my arms. No longer did we have one teacher for all subjects. Rather we students moved from classroom to classroom for each period's session. We also had lockers in the hallway in which we kept our wraps and books not needed for a given period. The high school offered an academic course for those hoping to go on to college. The other students could choose between a commercial course and a vocational course. I chose the academic program.

I could never get interested in history. I became impatient with the people we studied about who never seemed to learn to get along with each other. Also, there were too many dates to memorize. I didn't enjoy English literature classes either. To analyze stories spoiled them for me. We were also required to take two years of home economics. The first semester, during which we learned about food and food preparation, was interesting to me. The second semester, in which we learned sewing, was a real trial for me. I couldn't seem to make neat stitches, so had to keep pulling my work out and doing it over. As a result I never finished any project during the time allotted. At the end of the semester the teacher asked me where my finished products were. I replied that I had supposed that she had already failed me on them so I hadn't bothered to finish them. I got a D for the first year, and an F for the second year. That was the only failure I ever got.

On the other hand, I loved English grammar, including diagramming sentences. My English teacher taught both first-year and fourth-year English. There were blackboards all across the front and the right-hand side walls. The final exam questions for each of the two classes were written on the blackboards. The questions for the first-year students were on the front board. The questions for the fourth-year students were on the side board. It looked to me as though I could answer the questions for the fourth-year class also. Just for fun I asked the teacher to let me try taking the exam. She did so, and I got almost all of the questions right. Of course, this gave me great pride.

Likewise, I found Latin interesting and easy to catch onto. Naturally, I did exceptionally well. During my second year the teacher often gave me first-year Latin test papers to correct during class. Even so, I was able to follow what we were studying. When she called on me to answer a question, I was usually able to answer correctly.

Math classes were also interesting and challenging to me. It took several weeks to get the hang of algebra the first year, but soon I was able to understand without too much trouble. Likewise, it took me a few weeks to get the hang of geometry. General science classes were an eye-opener to me. The ways in which the sun, moon, stars, trees, plants, birds, animals, insects, rocks, etc., functioned in an orderly fashion began to come into focus and make sense. I really enjoyed these classes and did well in them.

Then there were the extra-curricular activities. I enjoyed athletics and was a moderately good player. In my third and fourth years I made the basket ball and volley ball teams which took part in competitions with other schools in the area. However, I had to wear a wire face mask while playing basketball, in which I played a guard position. In those days girls' basketball was different from boys' basketball. We had to stay in a given section of the court and weren't allowed to dribble the ball. We played field hockey in the fall. After the basketball and volleyball season was over, we learned archery, folk dancing, tap dancing, etc. It was all quite interesting to me.

The other exciting extracurricular activity was Girl Scouts. There was no scout program in the elementary school when I was growing up. This was new to me but it sounded interesting, so I joined the troop. I soon progressed to second class and then to first class and earned a dozen or more merit badges. The hiking and camping experiences were also very enjoyable.

My activities at church also changed. As mentioned earlier, I had been quite rambunctious in the junior Sunday School. Yet I seemed to be familiar with the Bible stories. For this reason I was asked to become a teacher of nine-year-old boys. My brother was in my first class, which made it an additional challenge, but I was excited to try it. It would channel some of my excess energy and enable me to serve the Lord in a tangible way. Our Sunday School used the Southern Baptist curriculum and training program. All teachers were expected to complete at least two training courses a year. This meant that I gradually learned the principles and methods of teaching children. I also took courses in Bible study and background on an adult level, all of which were helpful.

As a teenager I progressed to the Intermediate BYPU where soon I was elected president. Our leader at the time didn't play the piano and we hadn't learned how to sing without accompaniment. I wanted to do something about it, so I asked Mother to teach me a hymn. She chose a hymn in which the first, second, and fourth lines were exactly the same and which had simple music. She told me to figure out the right-hand music myself. After that she taught me the left-hand part. When I was able to play this hymn reasonably well, I told the group the next Sunday. They were so overjoyed that they sang it twice, once at the beginning and once at the end. This encouraged me to learn another hymn and then another. Gradually I learned to play common hymns quite well.

About two years later the DC Convention BYPU started monthly association meetings. All local groups were encouraged to send representatives. The Bible being the "Sword of the Spirit", we who were believers needed to learn how to use it. For example, we needed to learn how to find verses in the Bible quickly. So a monthly "Sword Drill" competition was started.. We would hold our Bibles with one hand on top of the Bible and one on the bottom. Our fingers were not to touch the edges of the Bible until the command, "Go." We would try to open the Bible as close as possible to the place where the verse would be found. Then we would quickly leaf through the remaining pages to where the verse was located. The first person to find it would step forward and start reading it. I enjoyed this very much and became quite proficient at it.

However, there was a sudden interruption to these varied experiences. My mother got sick and died in February of my first year of high school! She had known for several years before that she had diabetes. In those days the only known treatment was injecting insulin, and she hated it. Before injecting it, her urine first had to be tested in order to know how much to give her. So sometimes she refused to save it because she didn't want Daddy to give her an injection. She loved to cook and loved to eat, and found it very hard to stick to a diet. I can remember that she would succeed in dieting for as long as three weeks. Then she would go on a binge. She would fix herself gourmet sandwiches, etc., and gorge herself. In that way she undid all the good of the previous dieting. Finally, the doctor warned her and Daddy that there was a dangerous amount of sugar in her blood. He said that if she got even a mild sickness, it would probably result in taking her life.

That is exactly what happened. She got what appeared to be a grippe, which was a mild kind of flu, but became so ill that she was taken to the hospital. A few days later Daddy came home from the hospital looking very forlorn. He said to me that it looked as though Mother would never get well. I thought he meant that she would be an invalid all her life. I asked if she would come home or have to stay at the hospital. Then he said, "Your mother died." It was the only time I saw my father shed tears. My first reaction was to put my arm on his shoulder and try to comfort him. She was only thirty-seven years old. Of course, at first I didn't grasp the full significance of the difference it would make in our lives.

Duffy, my mother's older sister, soon came to stay with us. She took care of the house, meals, and us children. After several months she left. Years later, during my second furlough from the mission field, I was privileged to stay with her during her last week of life. One day she told me that she had thought I hated her. I asked her why and she explained. After my mother died, Daddy had asked her if she would consider marrying him. It would be for the sake of us children, even though he wouldn't be able to give her the same love he had given to Mother. So she came out for a trial stay. However, I had been very critical of her. I kept telling her that Mother didn't do things that way. She said that several times I told Daddy that Duffy had taken grocery money to use for herself. Obviously, she realized that it wouldn't work for her to marry Daddy. I was amazed to hear this. I assured her that I had no recollection of doing anything like that or of hating her for any reason. It must have been my natural reaction to my mother's death that I would resist anyone trying to take Mother's place.

Then I told her that as a child after Mother's death I had thought that Duffy hated me. The reason was as follows. My mother's youngest sister Katz went with us to the beach to look after us. One time when we got back, Duffy had found that all three of us children had head lice. She scolded me as the oldest child for not reporting it to Katz. As for me, I had never seen nor heard of head lice at that point. That was why I felt that I was blamed unfairly and so concluded that Duffy hated me. Then she in turn was amazed and she had no memory of it. Thus we both were able to get our misconceptions cleared up before she died.

After Duffy left our home, I cooked, bought groceries, and took care of the house as best as I could. Yet I also kept on with school and the extracurricular activities, so obviously I didn't do a very complete job. Also, I was limited to the foods I knew how to prepare. So as the new school year approached, Daddy began looking for a housekeeper. One Sunday afternoon he told us that a woman would be coming for an interview with him to see about becoming our housekeeper. My uncle Bryant and I stayed in the dining room and talked quietly while Daddy talked with the woman. I had been reading a lot of Horatio Alger's books at the time. In every one of them either the mother or the father died. After that, someone else would come into the life of the remaining spouse and be really nice to him/her and the children. Then after they got married, the children would be made miserable. So I told Bryant how worried I was that the same thing would happen in our case.

However, when Daddy did hire her, I tried my best to make her feel accepted and to explain our ways to her. Her name was Mrs. Major, and she was a widow with six children. Interestingly enough, her sister had married a Mr. Miner. This seemed amusing to us children even though her last name was not spelled with an "o". Mrs. Major was a lovely Christian woman and took good care of us all. I grew to love her and appreciate her very much. She was given an upstairs apartment as her living quarters. She remained with us for five years until her health broke down.

I was not aware of grieving for my mother. As indicated above, I guess I was resistant at first to anyone's trying to take my mother's place. However, with Mrs. Major's coming and proving to not be a Horatio Alger type of person, I was content. I returned to my active life at school and at the church. I believe that my brother was too young to realize much. It was my sister who seemed to take Mother's death the hardest of all. After all, she had been my mother's favorite and was close to her. She soon became attached to a Mrs. Pettit, who seemed to understand her and to fill the emptiness Then a year later, Mrs.

Pettit died. This was really hard on my sister. As for my father, he seemed to carry on as usual, and I didn't see any signs of his mourning. Of course, I am sure that he missed my mother a great deal.

I became interested in a craft correspondence course, and Daddy allowed me to take it. It consisted of one project each of about twelve different types of crafts. Directions and all needed materials to complete each project were included. When one project was finished, then another one would be sent. I learned to place a 9" x 5 1/2" piece of glass over a picture and copy it onto the glass using opaque water colors. This was the project I liked best. I also did a leather project; but I don't remember what the other projects were. Also, Daddy taught me how to show perspective in drawing.

I really wanted to live for the Lord and not do anything that would displease Him. Most of my church activities were either with children or with adults rather than with my peers. I often heard the adults criticize young people for their dating activities, so I got the impression that this was not pleasing to God. This was partly responsible for my having no interest in boys. Being so absorbed in the extracurricular activities at school was probably another reason. My father was not the type to show his emotions and I was like him in temperament. If my mother were still alive,, she probably would have guided me. Because of all of the above factors, I was very naive about boy-girl relationships.

Two incidents that I remember happened during this time. The church janitor was an African-American. In those days we called them "negroes". He was required to get to the church early on Sunday mornings. He had to unlock the doors, get the furnace going, etc. Then he had to stay there until the morning service was over to pick up trash, etc. After everyone had left, he was to lock the doors. In those days negroes were not allowed to sit in on the worship services. The church sanctuary had a balcony on one side with a number of Sunday School classrooms on the far side of the balcony. I believed that God wanted Christians to be friendly with all people. Whenever I met the janitor after the church service, I would always greet him and wish him well.

One of those times I had gone up to one of the classrooms after church and I met him. I greeted him as usual, and he responded by asking me if I would marry him. I was stunned, but assured him that I wasn't interested in marrying anyone. I thought it was rather amusing. Later I mentioned it laughingly to Lois Cook. She was the girl in high school I had become attached to. I never expected her to pass it on. She immediately told my father about it and he brought it to the deacons. They called the janitor and wanted to fire him. He pled with them not to do so, insisting that he hadn't touched me. That was true. He promised never to say any such thing to me again. My father never mentioned it to me. I learned it from Lois. Then I was embarrassed, and sorry for the poor janitor. The next time I saw him I apologized. I still greeted him, but he remained aloof.

As I walked to high school every day, I passed by my former third grade teacher's house. In my third year of high school I often saw her father in the yard and so I would greet him. One day he also proposed to me. I was shocked! I thought, "What is it about men that makes them think that if a girl greets them from time to time, she is in love with him?" Anyhow, I began to realize that I needed to be more careful in my relationships with men.

My last year of high school I was able to take typing as an elective, and that training has been extremely useful to me. Also, a few weeks after school started that year, I was asked if I would be interested in a special project. I would work in the library an hour a day instead of continuing with trigonometry. That sounded interesting to me, so I agreed. The librarian taught me about the Dewey Decimal System. She also showed me how to place books back in the proper places on the shelves. Sometimes she even had me make library cards for new books. Of course, in each case she also gave me the proper card number.

Toward the end of the school year there wasn't a great deal to do in the library. Then the librarian asked me to copy students' academic records onto new cards. Eventually I came to my own card and saw that F for Domestic Science. I began to wonder if it would be possible to make it up before the school year ended. I made a proposition to the Domestic Science teacher. If I made my graduation dress under her supervision, would she consider changing my F to at least a D. She agreed to let me try; but again and again my stitches didn't meet her approval. She was afraid that I might ruin the graduation dress. So she kept taking it and doing the sewing herself. As a result, I never dared to ask her to change my poor grade.

When Graduation Day finally came, it was an exciting time. In those days there was no special graduation ceremony upon the completion of elementary school. Thus, this was my first experience with all the pomp and ceremony. Although we didn't wear gowns, yet we wore a uniform type of clothing. We were given diplomas one by one. When awards were given out, I was quite surprised to have my name called. The American Legion gave an annual Citizenship Medal for the best all-round student. I had been chosen as the recipient for the medal. I am pleased that later both my sister and my brother received awards at their graduation. My sister was given an honorary award for excellence in typing. My brother was given the medal for excellence in scholarship.

Ever since my mother's death, her younger sister Katz went with us three children to our annual beach trip. Of course, she also took along her son Glenn who was just six months older than my little brother. The July that I turned seventeen years old something happened. All of us had learned to swim but not to dive. I saw other children diving off of the pier and it looked so easy. I wanted to try it, but was afraid that I would make a fool of myself. I didn't want anyone around while I tried to do it.

One afternoon the others went in from the water and nobody else was around. I saw my chance so I opted to stay a little longer and try diving. When I stood at the edge of the pier, I couldn't get up my courage enough to dive in. So I tried going back a way and then running to the end of the pier and diving in. This worked for three or four times. I decided to do it once more before going back to the hotel. However, this time just as I hit the water, my legs flipped backwards. I both heard and felt something crack, or so it seemed. I slowly got out of the water, and headed back. My back hurt, but I was able to walk all right. I told my aunt; but I seemed to be all right except for the pain, which was bearable. Having been a tomboy, I often bruised, scraped, or cut myself and just accepted the ensuing pain as a matter of course. I didn't think that much about it and neither did she. We were at the beach for another four or five days. I went ahead with everything as I had done before, although of course I didn't try any more diving.

After I got back home, I went to the family doctor because my back still hurt whether I was lying down, sitting up, or standing. He was getting along in years and was perhaps getting a bit senile. Anyway, he ordered a spoonful of Sodium Perborate in a glass of water three times a day. Strangely enough, it did seem to help for the first week, but not afterwards.

# COLLEGE AND NURSES TRAINING YEARS

College was a whole new experience! Most of the classes consisted of lectures on which the students were expected to take notes. There was often required outside reading as well. The tests were based on both the outside reading and the lectures. I got pretty good at taking notes using my own brand of abbreviations. The first two years were general . Then beginning in the third year students started on subjects connected with their major. I had opted to take nursing as my major. This would mean three more years of study before I would graduate with a B.S. degree

In the first two years of general courses, most subjects were required for all students. One of the requirements was two years of a foreign language. I discovered that Greek was offered. I thought that it would be useful for understanding the New Testament in the original version. It turned out that the professor lived two short blocks from the university campus. Classes were held at his home. There were only two of us in the class in the fall semester. Unfortunately, the professor got sick and died during the Christmas holidays. Then it was decided to discontinue the course; so I didn't get credit for it. The second semester of all language courses continued from what was taught in the first semester. Thus, It was not possible to enter any other language course in the second semester. This meant that I still had two more years of language study to complete before I could go into the nursing course.

My second year I took French, since I had studied it in high school. I had two choices for taking care of the second year of language. I could go to summer school and take a concentrated course of French. On the other hand, I could stay at the College Park campus another year. For various reasons it seemed better to remain at home one more year. For this third year in addition to the French, I could take any subjects I wanted to for which I had the prerequisites. I chose to take zoology, botany, and Home Management. For this latter course, the first semester we were taught the basic principles of good home management. In the second semester we actually lived together in a house on campus for six weeks. There were eight of us girls besides a teacher in the one house, and we changed jobs every four days.

The one who was manager was in charge of preparing the main part of each meal with the help of the assistant manager. The maid also assisted in the salad preparation. There were two housekeepers each with her tasks of cleaning and laundering spelled out. I don't remember what the other three jobs were. The manager and assistant manager planned the meals. They also ordered the food though they didn't have to go out and buy it themselves. On one of the days they had to plan a formal dinner which included a roast which needed to be carved. Both the manager and the assistant manager were each to invite one guest.

When it was my turn, I invited my father as my guest, and the assistant manager also invited someone. I had decided to serve a crown roast. It looked very nice with a decoration on the top of each rib bone. I thought that I did a pretty good job at carving it too. But when the maid removed the platter from the table, there was a ring of meat pieces on the tablecloth.

Fortunately, the maid was able to matter-of-factly use the crumber to brush them into the little tray that went with it. For each job the specific responsibilities were spelled out for us. It was a very good and practical experience.

The university had a clinic with a woman doctor in charge. Since my back still hurt, I went to the doctor to see what she thought was causing the pain. In those days X-Rays were seldom taken. It was generally understood that if one's back were broken in an accident, one would be paralyzed. So the doctor assumed that my problem was a muscle sprain. She ordered a camp corset to give support. It really felt good when I put it on. However, it was supposed to be held in place by attaching it to long stockings. I was ornery enough in those days that I refused to wear long stockings . When I put the corset on it felt good. But when I sat down it moved up. When I stood up again it didn't move back down. Then it was more uncomfortable than ever and I gave up using it. My back hurt the same whether I was standing up, sitting up, or lying down. When I was active, it didn't make it hurt any worse. So I went ahead and took part in all the sports at college. Being active helped me get my mind off the pain. Physical education was a required subject unless we had a doctor's order to not participate.

The university was two and a half miles from my home. My father worked in extension in the agricultural department there. When I started to college, he increased my allowance to twelve dollars a month to cover bus fare back and forth each school day. However, I preferred to walk and use the money for other things instead. It had become my habit to first set aside the tithe for the church. I mostly used the rest of it for books, as I loved to read. Once or twice when it was snowing hard, my father insisted that I go on the bus with him. He felt it was too dangerous for my health to walk there in the snowstorm.

One of the blessings of the university was the Baptist Student Union, abbreviated BSU. The DC Convention had a chapter on the University of Maryland campus. In addition to general meetings we were all urged to have a prayer mate. My prayer mate was Elizabeth Clarke, whom we called Betty. Her home was in Washington, DC, and she was also taking the five-year B.S. course with a major in nursing. We shared our personal fears and weaknesses as well as our concerns. We prayed about other people, events and situations, and really became close friends.

My first summer Betty invited me to go with her to the DC office to help fold and send out some notices. The BSU director, Howard Rees, chatted with me to get acquainted and help me feel at home. Then he started a series of summer weekly Bible discussions at the BSU office. On the very first evening as soon as I arrived, Howard greeted me by saying, "Emilie Ballard, I'm so glad to see you." I was really amazed and impressed that he remembered my name! I began to attend regularly and became a very active BSU-er. By the third summer, I became a leader of one of the Bible discussion groups. This meant another night each week in Washington for training in the Bible portion we would be discussing.

The Southern Baptist Convention had their national camp grounds at Ridgecrest. NC. I believe it was during the second summer that I went there with Betty for the week of the BSU assembly. They had worship and activity sessions following breakfast. Then there were two guest speakers who gave lectures on topics of interest to college-age students. Both of them were extremely interesting and inspiring. The first one was on developing our spiritual lives. The second one was on guidance in choosing and developing relationships with the opposite sex.

When I entered the meeting hall for the first lecture, I saw on the platform the ugliest man I had ever seen! He was short and humped over, had enormous ears, and the heel of one of his shoes was built up about three inches. He looked to me like a monster! How could I get anything out of his lecture? I was afraid that I wouldn't be able to stop thinking about his looks. But when he stood up to speak, there was an aura about him, a light emanating from his face. Also, his words were obviously spoken in the power of the Holy Spirit. Immediately I forgot what he looked like and was lifted to spiritual heights myself.

I took detailed notes on the lectures of both speakers. After I returned home, I wrote them up and made mimeographed copies. I distributed them to folks at my church, and they were a blessing to many.

Before Mother died, Daddy and she had talked about building a new house on the north side of our property. We children were growing up and our house was getting a bit crowded. After she died, I thought that the plans had been dropped. However, in early 1937 Dad began drawing up plans for the new house. We three children were still living at home, and we also had a live-in housekeeper.

The actual construction began later the same year, and we moved into it in early 1938. It was built on the edge of the hill which ran from south to north near the middle of the property. That meant that the first floor was on the ground level in the front. The basement, however, was on the ground level at the back. It contained a large recreation room as well as a furnace room and a storage room. The house was built of beautiful stones of pleasing browns, grays, and whites about twelve inches square each and sat in the midst of some tall oak trees which had been protected from the construction activity. As far as I know, it is still lived in by someone today.

The new housekeeper, Mrs. Carrie Flickinger, was the mother of my good high school friend, Lucy Flickinger. She was a widow and had six children and several grandchildren at that time. We all liked her very much. She seemed to care about our family members and the house. She also joined our church and became active in both the church and the community. She stayed with us for a number of years, leaving only when her health failed and she had to go into a nursing home.

I continued my interest in scouting during the three years of college. I served as lieutenant of two Girl Scout troops and acting captain of a third. During my first year I won a poster contest carried out by the county Girl Scouts but sponsored by the local Horticulture Society.

During July and August a day camp was held at our new area campgrounds about five miles from my home. Once I learned the way, I began roller skating to and from the camp, at which I served as a counselor. I believe we had two week-end overnights for the girls who were working on advanced merit badges. At the overnights we taught them how to build shelters and furniture by lashing. We also taught them how to find wood dry enough to burn after rainy weather, and how to build and start a fire without matches. A Seventh Day Adventist couple lived on property adjoining our camp grounds and they had some goats. These were interesting for the girls to watch, as they had not seen live goats before.

One day I was gathering dead branches from some of the trees for firewood on the hill above the camp buildings,. I inadvertently stepped into a hornet's nest attached to a dead branch which had broken off and fallen to the ground. When I began to feel the burning stings of the hornets on my legs, I looked down and saw what the cause was. I had the presence of mind to just freeze as I was. The hornets continued to fly around but didn't sting me anymore as long as I kept still. Then one of the campers began to come up the hill to help me carry the firewood. I called out to her not to come any farther because of the hornets. I tried to speak without moving my lips any more than necessary. However, one of the hornets was close to my face and stung my lip. After waiting perhaps another fifteen or twenty minutes, the hornets finally settled down into their nest again. I slowly extricated myself and was able to return without any further trouble. Fortunately, I was not allergic to their venom and my ankles and lip healed in a couple of days.

During my third year of college a Southern Baptist missionary doctor named Dr. John Lake came to Hyattsville on his furlough. The wife and children made their home there and attended our church regularly. He was usually away speaking at one church or another on Sundays. However, one Sunday he spoke at our church and made a tremendous impression on me!

He was a missionary doctor to China. He had become concerned about the many lepers in the rural areas who were not getting treated. Not only were they not getting better, they were infecting more and more people with the disease. Once it was obvious that their skin was leprous, they were banned from their villages. The banned lepers banded together and lived lonely lives in the jungle areas. There was an island off the coast of the Yantze River. Dr. Lake asked permission from the government to build a hospital for the lepers on it. He also wanted to build a community of huts where they could live with some of their fellow lepers as well as any family members who were also leprous. The government was willing to grant permission. However, it warned him that a band of robbers lived on one end of the island. Dr. Lake went to visit the robber chief and asked him if they would help him build these structures. He promised to pay them a decent wage and they agreed.

The island was twelve miles long and a half mile wide at its widest point. The hospital had an assembly room which was also used for Sunday worship. It had a balcony at the back where non-lepers could sit and worship together with the leper community. Often the robbers would attend the services. Many of them later became born-again Christians.

Every week Dr. Lake went out to the jungle areas looking for leper groups in hiding there. He offered them food, lodging, and treatment if they would let him take them to the island. I remember his telling us about one time when he started to enter a jungle area. He was stopped by a robber who put a gun to his chest and said, "I am going to kill you." Dr. Lake replied in a calm voice, "Well, if you kill me, I'll get to Heaven quicker than you get to Hell." The robber was so surprised at his reply and his lack of fear, that he turned on his heel and left him.

Dr. Lake's talk made a deep impression on me, and reinforced my desire to become a foreign missionary. I had gotten pretty good at taking notes on college lectures, so I took notes on his talk. Later I wrote them up and made mimeographed copies for the worshipers at the church.

The University had five schools in Baltimore. They were the School of Medicine, the School of Nursing, the School of Dentistry, the School of Pharmacy, and the School of Law. The first four used the University Hospital there as the place for the practical side of the training.

I entered the nursing course the first week of October, 1939. We class members were on probation for six months. After that the decision would be made as to whether we showed promise of becoming good nurses or not. The probationers wore blue pin-striped uniforms with white aprons, collars, cuffs, and caps. All student nurses wore black stockings and shoes. In those days nobody else wore black stockings, so we hated them. The graduate nurses wore white stockings and shoes.

The nurses' home was behind the hospital. We were fortunate to be in a fairly new building and everything was lovely there. Most of the student nurses smoked when they were off-duty. Fortunately, my roommate, Tillie Logan, did not. It was the custom there to call everyone by their last names, so I was called Ballard.

During the first few months we usually had three hours of classes Monday through Saturday. Those of us who had taken the pre-nursing course at the University in College Park were exempt from courses which we had already studied. Instead, we worked in the hospital the extra hours.

I liked most of the courses, especially Anatomy and Physiology, Bacteriology, and Nursing Procedures. I didn't care for Materia Medica which was about the use of medications nor the History of Nursing. In Nursing Procedures, we learned various techniques and practiced on each other.

We also had one and a half hours of ward work Monday through Saturday and three hours on Sundays. At first the ward work was mostly in Central Supply. We did cleaning, and also put clean linen away. Sometimes we folded bandages or wrapped supplies to be sterilized. Later, as we learned various nursing procedures, we began working with patients.

The first three to four months of our training were spent mostly in class work. After that we began working on the wards most of the time. We made beds, delivered meal trays, fed patients who couldn't feed themselves, and bathed patients in bed.

I had gotten into bad habits in my high school and college years. i had been doing so much volunteer work that I didn't have time to do my best. Still, I was appreciated and praised. So I had become satisfied with less than my best possible performance . But in nurses' training it was not enough to be willing. It was important to strive for perfect performance since patients' lives would be involved. So it was that again and again I thought that I had practiced procedures enough. But I was often unable to perform correctly in class when called upon.

As a result, when I was working on the wards, the supervisors seemed to pick on me often. Also, I seemed to have a mental block of some sort on the wards. My assignments were supposed to be completed between seven and nine-thirty a.m. Yet it always seemed to take me until eleven a.m. to finish. Part of it was because I cared about the patients. I spent time trying to help them to not be afraid or worried.

The second week of November I went into business in my spare time, darning silk stockings at a nickel a pair. If I charged any more, nobody would give me any business. By May some of the graduate nurses began giving me their stockings to darn also. The third week of November there was no work for us to do on the wards. Then several of us were asked to help fix up the library. There I spent my time making catalog cards for all of the books and magazines.

Before I had left for nurses training, my father had recommended that I move my church membership to the Seventh Baptist Church. He had attended there several times and knew that the minister preached from the Bible. However, I discovered that it was clear on the other side of the city from where I was. It took a half hour by bus to get there. Nevertheless, I joined the church and received a blessing from it. Everyone was very friendly.

In December I was in a church Christmas pageant. And in January I played the organ for the hymn singing in the chapel during the regular pianist's month of night duty. So, my past experiences and training came in handy. It enabled me to be useful away from the wards occasionally.

Beginning with our fourth month we were given two-day leaves once a month. On one of those breaks, which was during Doris's mid-semester vacation, I went to Frederick, MD, to visit her at Hood College. On another one, I visited Mary Franklin in Clinton, where she was studying at the time.

The middle of February about thirty nurses were off-duty because of respiratory infections. Many of the old people at the church were also home sick or caring for family members who were sick. Even the pastor was sick. Probably it was a flu epidemic, but we didn't know much about epidemics in those days. Of course it meant extra work for those of us nurses who were not sick, but we managed somehow.

As the end of the probation period neared, I began to be concerned that I might not be accepted. If that should happen, how could I face people at home again? But by God's grace, they accepted me and continued to work with me. After a year and a half, I suddenly became able to complete my work in good time. Evidently the mental block had disappeared. After I graduated, one nurse told me that there for awhile she thought I wouldn't make it.

The middle of July I went on night duty for the first time. The first week I was unable to sleep more than four hours during the day. Then I got adjusted and was able to sleep from eight or nine a.m. until four p.m. without waking up.

Once I became accustomed to night duty, I began taking a correspondence art course. I enjoyed it very much and soon became quite proficient. In fact, many of the nurses decided to buy their Christmas cards from me.

One night I had a little excitement. A new patient from the county with Rocky Mountain Spotted Fever disappeared about 1 a.m. We searched the wards on that floor as well as the stairs with no success. She was finally found on the floor in her room under a pneumonia patient's bed.

In November of my second year I was able to get to the State BSU Convention in College Park. I had wanted to go because my sister Doris had been asked to give the devotional. I was very proud of her.

My BSU prayer mate, Betty Clarke, was a year ahead of me in nurses' training. We resumed our prayer times together until she graduated two years later. This helped me to be receptive to the Spirit's working in me and on my behalf.

After probation we spent three months on each of the different types of wards. This continued up until our third year. During my three months on the general medical ward we had an unusual case. A man was admitted who had a fungus infection of the skin all over his body. I have never seen another case like it in my life time. No treatment for it was known. They just treated the symptoms as best as they could. As the fungus broke down, it exuded a sticky fluid which smelled up the whole place. They ended up vacating one whole wing of all other patients as long as he was there. The nurses only went over when necessary to treat him or give him medication. I felt sorry for him, and have often wondered what happened to him. He must have felt extremely lonely and forlorn.

I had another unusual experience during my time on that ward: A woman was admitted who had an advanced case of diabetes. One night she went into insulin shock . I quickly carried out the instructions to offset it. Later, she complained to the nursing supervisor that I had stolen her wedding ring. Of course, I hadn't and nobody else believed that I had. Still, it was nowhere to be found. I don't know whether it was ever found for they didn't assign that patient to me anymore.

During my time on the pediatrics ward there was a cute little boy about five years old. He had a hyperactive thyroid. His eyes bulged out and it was hard to keep him still. There was also a six-month-old infant girl nearby who was skin and bones. She crossed one leg over the other the way a person sitting in a chair crosses his/her leg. We would try to straighten her legs out. Each time she would slowly bend her knees and cross her legs again. The doctors didn't seem to know what caused this child to develop so abnormally, and didn't know how to treat it.

For some reason the boy with the hyperactive thyroid took a fancy to her. He kept wanting to climb into her crib. The nurses tried to find a way to keep the boy in bed, finally strapping him down. But one night I discovered that the boy had the baby girl in bed with him. He must have managed to struggle out of his restraints. Then somehow he had evidently managed to climb into the girl's crib. Then he took her out and carried her into his own bed. We were all amazed at his accomplishment, but of course, he couldn't be allowed to do that again. They ended up locking him up strapped to his bed in a small room. It seemed cruel, but they didn't know what else to do. I was transferred to another ward soon after that, but I have often wondered about them.

In my third year we had three months each in four more specialized nursing set-ups. There was three months of psychiatric nursing at St Elizabeth's Insane Asylum. For three months we were in charge of a ward. We also had three months in public health home visiting service. The last kind of training for me was in the operating room for three months.

The three months in psychiatric nursing was really an eye-opener! For one thing I discovered that most mental cases usually seemed quite normal. There would be just one aspect of their minds which was abnormal. I also found that many of them were very smart. The first thing we learned was that we had to wear a key on a strong cord around our waists. Every door was kept locked. We had to be able to unlock doors while carrying things and immediately lock them again. The milder cases could mingle with each other in the dining room or lounge. More violent cases were kept locked in individual rooms, often with no furniture. Most of our time was spent in one of two ways. We helped with treatments and we also provided occupation or entertainment for the patients. We sometimes made posters announcing events or favors to give the patients on special occasions.

We had classes on mental disorders every week day to help us understand about the patients' conditions . We were given the easier patients to care for at first. Only the last month were we given assignments with the more violent cases. During my last month I got my glasses broken twice by the same violent patient each time. Plastic lenses had not yet been invented. New glasses were provided to us quickly free of charge. I was supposed to unlock this patient's door, set the tray of food down on the floor inside quickly, and immediately lock the door again. But she sometimes waited beside the door. Then while I was setting the tray down, she caught hold of my glasses, causing them to fall to the floor. The regular nurses were experienced. They managed to sweep up the broken glass before the patient hurt herself with it. They also retrieved my glasses frame. I appreciated what I learned from this three months. However, I am sure that I would never want to do this kind of work full time.

I started my public health nursing in May of my last year. I found it extremely interesting although there was a lot to learn in this course. In those days there were no nursing homes like nowadays. There were only old folks homes which were sad places that nobody wanted to go to. They were the last resort for old folks who had nobody to care for them. So public health nurses served much as visiting health nurses do in our time. We also visited various clinics and other projects. This acquainted us with organizations which were providing services for those whose health was failing. I rather enjoyed the three months in public health nursing, but of course, we were given the easier cases.

My operating room experience came the last three months before I completed my training. In the operating room we first served as a circulating nurse. We got whatever sterile supplies were needed by the operating team. We picked up whatever fell on the floor. We discarded whatever was waste. We dropped whatever would be needed for operations into sterilizing solution. Later on we learned to be a scrub nurse. We first scrubbed our hands and arms thoroughly with a brush. Then we dried them with a sterile towel and put on sterile gloves. After this we were not supposed to touch anything unsterile.

A skilled scrub nurse would have learned the way the surgeons worked. Hence they were able to anticipate whatever the surgeon was going to need next. They would slap it into his hand before he had to ask for it. His gloves deadened the feeling in his hand a bit. Also, he was not looking at his hand but at the operation site. That is why things had to be slapped into his hand hard enough for him to feel it. The hospital was the practical training ground for both nursing and medical students. Thus the surgeons got used to having inexperienced trainees helping on the team. I was finally able to do a passable job but wouldn't want to be an operating room nurse as a graduate.

In May of my third year the Seventh District Association of churches held a "Better Speakers Contest". I decided to participate. My topic was "Transformed in the Image of Christ". I had been having some wonderful spiritual experiences . Christ was very real to me during that period of time. I didn't win, but it was a good experience.

The University's commencement exercises took place on the first Saturday of June. The graduating nurses were allowed to attend the Corporate Communion. It took the place of the Baccalaureate Service in College Park. The next morning we were taken to the College Park campus in a reserved bus . Those of us who were taking the five-year course sat with the Arts and Science division at first. After receiving our B.S. diplomas we moved over to where the rest of the graduating nurses were seated. When it was our turn, we went up again to get our nursing diplomas. However, the nursing supervisor took our diplomas from us on the return trip to Baltimore. She would keep them until we had completed the full three years of nurses training on October third, 1944. At that time all of the graduating nurses were given their nursing certificates. Those of us who had taken the five-year course were also given our B.S. diplomas again. However, before we could become registered nurses (R.N.s), we would still need to take a government exam . It would cover all aspects of our training. It was usually given near the end of the calendar year.

In the meantime, the United States had entered World War II. Army nurses were badly needed, so we were allowed to take the government exam before graduation if we chose. I and one other nurse, Gladys Foster, opted to do so, and we passed it. This meant that we were eligible to enter the armed service immediately upon completing our training.

The nursing superintendent had already interviewed all of the members of our graduating class. She wanted to know about our plans following graduation. She strongly felt that we owed it to the hospital to work there for a few years after graduation. The only exception she approved of was to go into the armed service because of the war. Since another class would graduate in just four more months, I decided to stay at the hospital for the four months. I would then join the Army Nurse Corp.

I was assigned to the Delivery Room, an assignment which I quite enjoyed. In those days women came to the hospital to have their deliveries. If it was a first pregnancy, they were told to wait until their contractions were five minutes apart. If they had had previous deliveries, they should come in when they first began having contractions. Their primary care physicians examined them regularly during their pregnancy. If they expected a problem, they were instructed to go to the hospital sooner.

The babies were kept in a nursery, which was also the responsibility of the delivery room nurses. They were taken out to the mothers in the maternity wards when it was time for them to be nursed. The mothers usually remained in the hospital for seven to ten days before discharge. If the babies had been born prematurely or for some other reason were not healthy, they were kept longer. Otherwise, they would be discharged along with their mothers.

I remember one woman in particular. She was a large African-American woman who had come to the hospital for two previous pregnancies. In both cases the babies were too large to come through the birth canal. They had to crush the baby in order for the mother to live. If they tried to save the baby, the mother would die from exhaustion. They didn't think it wise to do a Caesarian section on someone who was already having strong contractions. Her babies were destroyed both times. The second time the mother was told that she should plan to have a Caesarian Section the next time.

I was in the delivery room when she had this operation. Her baby was a healthy boy weighing thirteen pounds. He was so far developed that he looked like a three-months-old baby. He had a head full of black kinky curls and we sometimes tied bow ribbons in his hair. When I was taking the babies out to be nursed, I sometimes took this one around for the other mothers to see. Needless to say, both the mother and her husband were overjoyed at having this delightful baby boy.

That was an enjoyable four months; but when it ended, I was ready to venture out into the world. I wanted to work as a graduate nurse away from the supervision of the hospital where I had trained.

# ARMY DAYS

When I left the employ of the University Hospital, I went promptly to the Army headquarters in Baltimore. There on February eighth, 1943, I enlisted in the Army Nurse Corps. I was told to report to Camp Beale near Marysville in northern California on the fifteenth. They assured me that someone from the camp would meet me at the Marysville train station. I was allowed to take only one foot locker and one bedroll besides my purse.

I returned home to get ready and to purchase needed articles and get train tickets. I learned that it would take four nights and three days to get there, so I planned accordingly. My home church, the First Baptist Church of Hyattsville, had a going away party prior to my departure. They had a time of prayer for me and dedication of me as their own missionary. Each person present wrote me a letter to be read along the way.

I left in the evening from the depot in Washington, DC. I travelled by coach class facing in the direction the train was going. Being winter, snow covered the ground most of the way. The dining car was six cars back, so I got a bit of exercise going to meals three times a day. The lowest priced dinner cost ninety cents, but it was quite good. I had a total of forty letters, so I portioned them out over the five days. I read five of them Monday evening. Then I read ten on each of the next three days. That left five for Friday morning. I became acquainted with a soldier in the same car i was in. He was returning to Camp Beale, and he described the camp set-up to me. This

47

helped prepare me for the shock of wooden barracks. He told me that the nurses' basic training lasted thirteen weeks.

The scenery was interesting since my knowledge of the geography of the land was limited. After all, I had never travelled west of Maryland since I was seven years old. After leaving Chicago the second day, we came to the Rocky Mountains early in the evening. The next day I wrote quite a few Hyattsville folks planning to mail my postcards in Salt Lake City. I told them that we had left the Rocky Mountains behind and were approaching Salt Lake City. However, the next evening we passed through about as many mountains as we had the day before! We went through two tunnels, one of which was six miles long and the other two miles long. In the tunnels the smoke from the engine worked its way into the cars making it hard to breathe. It also coated the outside of the windows so we couldn't see very well the rest of the trip. The train bypassed Sacramento and arrived in Marysville six hours late at eight-twenty a.m.

Marysville appeared to be slightly larger than Hyattsville. It was a thrill seeing everything green when we woke up that morning. We saw real oranges ripening on the trees, as well as apple and peach orchards and grape vineyards. Someone was waiting at the station with a sign saying Camp Beale, and took me to the camp. Camp Beale was nine miles away. Bus service between Marysville and Camp Beale was provided every hour during the day. The camp officially opened the previous October. Two girls arrived from New York in the evening, and the three of us were oriented together.

Two Army nurses, Ruth Venemon and Peggy (?) were Presbyterian and very active Christians. Ruth visited me the first evening as I was unpacking my bedroll and making my bed.

Gertrude Emerson Long-

Engagement Picture

Mother and Daddy

Soon after Marriage

Mother Holding Emilie

In Mother's Babye Dress

L to R– Emilie, Walter, Arthur, Gertrude and Doris

Emilie, Arthur, Doris

Before Haircuts

Emilie, Arthur, Doris

After Haircuts

Mothers Father,

Joseph M. Long

Mother's Mother

Ida Snell Long

Mother's Oldest Sibling

Dorothy Duffy Long

Mothers Oldest Brother

Hallock P. Long

Mother's Second Oldest Brother

George Long

Killed in World War I

Carleton Long

His Wife,

Dorothy Fisher Long

Katherine Long Bartoo

Bernard Bartoo

Bryant Alden Long

His wife, Dorothy Jane

Gertrude Ballard Mitchelson

Her Husband, Roy Mitchelson

Emilie as a Nurse Student

Emilie as an Army Nurse

Emilie as a Missionary

Emilie as a Retiree

Besides the bed, the only other item of furniture was an orange crate standing up on end beside the bed. I had put a small framed picture of Christ in Gethsemane on top of the orange crate. Seeing it, she invited me to go with her and her friend to the worship service at the camp chapel the next day. I had stopped praying and going to church during my last year at the University Hospital. Yet I still wanted to become strong in my faith again. Since I didn't know anyone at the camp, I was glad to accept her invitation. These two girls were taking Moody Bible Institute correspondence courses, so I was inspired to do so also. I took one on Survey of the Bible and one on Scripture Memorizing. Both of them were very helpful and informative. Soon I was active in my faith once again.

Camp Beale was a camp for units heading for overseas service. They were mostly field artillery, tank, and tank destroyer units. The hospital mostly had the boys who got sick or were injured at the camp. I was assigned to a ward that was for contagious diseases. Interestingly enough the diseases being then treated were measles and mumps. A number of fellows from the south had never had these childhood diseases. Then they succumbed to them at the camp. The wards had seventy-five beds each. For awhile, there were three wards of measles cases and two wards of mumps cases. Several months later after the measles and mumps cases had been cured, we got about eighty soldiers with malaria. They had been in Guadalcanal and New Caledonia.

The ward doctor was a German who had fled to America early in Hitler's reign. When he came on duty, he would call out, "Miss Bah-yar, where are you?" He pronounced the double "l" in my last name as a "y" and put the stress on the second syllable.

In addition to our ward work, we had several hours of basic army training. Mostly we learned the protocol. We learned how to salute. We learned to snap to attention and salute an officer with a higher rank. We learned to obey orders immediately. It didn't matter whether we did or didn't understood why the order was given. We learned how to march in formation both in left-right unison and in route step.

Of course, I became active in the work of both the post chapel and the hospital worship service. After having completed the thirteen weeks of basic training, I was able to do other things. I began to take lessons on the Hammond organ at the chapel . It was about one mile away from the hospital area. I worked in the nurses' victory garden between two of our barracks. I also helped the Red Cross recreation worker at the hospital.

One Sunday we had communion at the chapel service. When I started to drink the grape juice from the little communion cup, I found that it was wine. It tasted awful to me. Furthermore, when I was about eleven years old I had joined the Loyal Temperance League. As a result, I had signed a pledge to never drink, sell, or offer alcoholic beverages. I couldn't finish drinking from my communion glass, and in my heart prayed to the Lord to forgive me. After the service, I spoke to the chaplain about it. I asked whether it seemed important to him to use wine rather than grape juice. He replied that while it wasn't necessary, in his church they had always used it. I told him that in the Baptist Church to which I belonged, alcoholic beverages were forbidden. After that, he used grape juice instead.

The work of the army nurse is mostly supervision and book work. The medical corps men do most of the actual work. An inspection was held once a month. We did our best to have everything dusted, orderly, and spic and span. The officer who came around to do the inspection was quite big and tall. There was a tall cupboard which we had carefully dusted. Yet he was so tall that he was able to wipe a bit of dust off onto his white glove. After he left, I climbed up onto a chair to see where he had found the dust. I discovered a small triangle of dust that we had missed but that the tall officer had been able to see.

One day we were not very busy, so I and the corps men began scrubbing the walls. Before long, the nursing supervisor came in and saw me scrubbing along with the corps men. She promptly scolded me- I was supposed to supervise, and have the corps men do the work. That is not my nature! I knew then that I would never make army nursing my career. It was a fairly new thing to have women in the army. However, before the War men didn't train as nurses. They first took in army nurses, and then a little later began the WAC training. Doctors and nurses were automatically taken into the service as officers I started as a second lieutenant. Also, they were not forced to go overseas. Rather, requests were posted on the bulletin board every so often asking for volunteers. I was eager to go overseas. Being young, it seemed as though it would be an adventure. Besides, that was where nurses were needed the most. However, they were afraid to let me go because of my poor eyesight. They said that if my glasses got broken, I would be more of a liability than an asset.

Ruth and Peggy, my good friends, were sent overseas after five months. However, before they left, God had brought another strong Christian nurse to fellowship with me. By the time she was sent overseas, 'God had provided still another nurse who was a strong Christian. God did this for the entire eighteen months that I was at Camp Beale. It was not common for army personnel to be strong, outgoing Christians. Thus, I consider this to be a miracle of God on my behalf to build up my faith.

Deep in my heart I really didn't want to go overseas unless God wanted me to. Yet, with every request for volunteers, I felt compelled to tell my sad story in the mess hall . I said that I wanted to go, but they wouldn't have me. I prayed about it often. I thought that I was accepting the situation as God's will for me; yet it wasn't so. I still wanted to tell folks that they wouldn't accept me. Finally, after a year and five months, I succeeded. I got to the point where I really didn't want to go overseas if it wasn't God's will.

Then, believe it or not, two weeks later everything changed! Nurses were needed overseas very badly! It was rumored that if you could see two yards in front of you with one eye they would accept you. So I was accepted and two weeks after that I departed for overseas! Isn't that just like God to wait patiently for one to come to the point of really choosing God's will. Then God turns around and gives the very thing one had wanted!

We were sent to Italy in a hospital ship. As soon as the sun went down, no light was allowed outside the cabins, not even lighted cigarettes. An enemy submarine might see it and torpedo the ship. There were two sets of doors for going out on deck. We opened the first one and closed the door behind us before opening the second one to the outside. . The ship had to zigzag quite a bit in order to avoid being hit by a torpedo from an enemy submarine. This slowed us down quite a bit but eventually we arrived at Naples.

I was glad to find that I didn't get seasick. However, we nurses had to take turns caring for patients in the sick bay down in the hold. Down there the air was very close and the ship's motion very noticeable . This made it hard for us to control ourselves.

There were twelve of us nurses on board. We were to be replacements for nurses of the Seventh Station Hospital killed in the North African Campaign. We spent a week in Naples waiting for the Seventh Station Hospital unit to arrive. Then it was another week before we were transferred up north.

Shortly after I arrived in Naples, I met a Red Cross worker also expecting to join the Seventh Station Hospital. She had arrived a few days before I did. There was a hill rising above the town of Naples on which there was a row of cameo shops. Cameo brooches and other kinds of ornaments were made from pieces of shell. They usually pictured women's heads. The Red Cross worker had persuaded one of the craftsmen to allow her to make her own cameo. When she told me about it, I wanted to try it also. She persuaded him to take me on as well. It was good advertising for the shop. Soldiers walking along outside could see us through the big window. They would come into the shop to talk with us. Then they would look at the cameos on display and often buy one or more.

The process of making a cameo was very interesting. The inner side of shell is a tan or rose color. The rough outside layer had already been removed by the craftsmen. Also, the bits of shell had already been cut up into small circles or ovals. The picture was made by chiseling off bits of the pink or tan inside layer until the deeper white layer showed through. The piece to be worked on was fastened onto the end of a thick stick with putty . The side of the stick was then braced firmly against the side edge of the table. A tiny chisel was used to remove the portions of the inner layer not wanted.

I opted to make a scene rather than a woman's head. I had a ship's sail showing on the water with mountains in the background . Then I had a bird flying above near a cloud. We only worked half a day, so It took me two days to complete it. Then it had to be polished with linseed oil. I didn't bother to get it mounted, but kept it as a memento. Just for fun, I asked the shopkeeper what he thought it might be worth. He estimated two lire, which is less than a penny.

We were transported by army trucks to Livorno, called Leghorn in English. It is a little bit around the bend of the boot of Italy east of Genoa. Our hospital was to be set up in a C-shaped cement building. Mussolini had used it as a training school for Fascist youth.

There are several types of army hospitals. The field hospital is right at the edge of the tents for the men actually fighting. It keeps patients no longer than twenty-four hours. The evacuation hospital is a little farther back from the field and has a capacity of two hundred beds. It keeps patients for just a few days. Those that can be sent quickly back into the fight are returned. Those who need more extensive treatment are sent on to the nearest station hospital. Station hospitals usually have a capacity of five hundred patients. Those who are expected to need prolonged treatment are sent on to a general hospital. Such hospitals usually have a capacity of one thousand patients.

A general hospital and an evacuation hospital were already set up and functioning in Leghorn. However, it was the time of the big push through the Po Valley. The Italian soldiers were surrendering en masse as they realized that they couldn't win. They had also heard that the American Army didn't kill prisoners of war. Therefore, both of those two hospitals were overloaded. We were told that we had better set up for seven hundred fifty patients instead of just five hundred. The first day that we opened, we received twelve hundred! The patients were coming in so fast that we all kept busy until evening. We didn't think to have some nurses go and get some rest before coming on night duty. At five p.m. we realized that some of us were going to have to continue working the whole night. I was one who volunteered to do so. Because there was so much to do, we had no trouble staying awake.

In a few weeks we received twelve German prisoners of war. They had to be guarded at all times. Fortunately, there was a room across from the nurses' station which was large enough to accommodate them. The guard only had to be at the entrance to the room. Of course, we couldn't speak their language and they didn't know English. However, with the aid of the charts sent along with the patients and using gestures, we were able to care for them. Within a few weeks they were all transferred farther behind the lines . Those who were cured were sent to a prisoners-of-war camp. Those who needed further treatment were sent to a general hospital.

The Brazilian Army was allied with the American Fifth Army in Italy. Most Americans in the USA at that time didn't realize that. About two months after we opened the Seventh Station Hospital, we became designated as the Brazilian Hospital. Brazilian army doctors and medical corps men were assigned to work alongside our American army staff. About two weeks later twelve Brazilian "hostess-interpreter" girls were added to the staff. Since they spoke no English, it seemed as though their function was to build up the morale of the Brazilian soldiers. We nurses were living in tents, four to a tent. The tents had not been winterized and the weather was getting colder all the time. The Brazilian officer in charge of these girls insisted that their tents needed to be winterized. So of course, our tents got winterized along with theirs. The top and the sides were reinforced with an extra heavy layer . We also got pot-bellied stoves, one in the middle of each tent.

I started studying advanced piano from a soldier who was an expert pianist. He was reluctant to teach me because he said he lost patience easily. I persuaded him to teach me anyhow. On the other hand, I started teaching my assistant chief nurse beginning piano and she seemed to catch on fairly easily. I also started studying Italian, but actually I used Portuguese more. This was because by then nearly two-thirds of our patients were Brazilian. I was on night duty for awhile and one of the Brazilian patients started teaching me.

The Brazilian army provided a Catholic chaplain since it is a Catholic country. However, it allowed a seminary student from a Baptist seminary in Brazil who was in the army there to hold Protestant services. I was glad to help out by playing the little pump field organ for the Protestant services. By March I had started memorizing Scripture verses in Portuguese.

About a month later I had a chance to witness to the Brazilian army medical officer on my ward. It happened like this: He asked me why I always seemed so happy. I thought that it wasn't proper to talk about Christian beliefs while on duty. So I simply replied that perhaps I'd tell him later. He asked me again a few days later. This time I made a date to meet with him outside the hospital in the afternoon after I had gone off duty. I told him about God's plan for salvation as best as I could. Using a Brazilian New Testament which I had, I got him to read the verses out loud. He said that in all his forty plus years no one had ever said anything to him about the condition of his soul. Although I don't speak Portuguese very well, he said that he understood everything which I told him very well. I know that the Holy Spirit was responsible.

I had several more talks with him, and then he surprised me by asking me to marry him. I nearly fell over! I tried to explain to him that I loved him as a friend because God wants us to love everyone that way. But I said I didn't love him with the kind of love that wanted to marry him. He couldn't seem to grasp my explanation. I guess that in Brazil marriage is not based on a love relationship at all. He was disappointed. As for me, I was sorry that he had misunderstood my wanting to spend time talking with him. I didn't meet with him again, and before long he was transferred back to Brazil.

For Christmas the Red Cross promoted a contest between the wards. They provided red and green crepe paper, tissue paper, and construction paper from their limited supply. We discovered two patients on our ward who had studied art. They were willing to take charge of the planning and did most of the art work. The other patients helped out with the rest of the decorating. There was a partition which ran down the middle of the ward lengthwise which was about four feet high. Every so often there was a pillar extending from it to the ceiling. Between each of them the boys painted the flag of some allied nation. These included China, Burma, and India. One of the patients had received a V-mail which contained authentic messages in the respective languages. These were copied down under the flags.

The partition was about six inches thick, which made a ledge at the top. Someone found some pots and transplanted some shrubbery from outside near the windows. These were set up on the ledge. In an open space along the other wall they placed a creche. On either side of that a real wooden candlestick containing five candles each was placed. Around on the walls were pictures made by some of the patients. Wreaths were made from bunches of pine sprigs bound together. Small bunches of berries from a nearby shrub were then inserted. Altogether the decorations were quite impressive, and we won the first prize! The hospital staff members went Christmas caroling the two nights before Christmas, half of the staff each night. We also had special Christmas worship services.

Beginning in February the work had settled into a routine, so we were given one day a week off. I started working in the Special Service library helping set it up and cataloging the books. I decided to work on that project on my day off for three weeks each month. Then on the fourth week I took a trip to Florence or some other place of interest. My first trip was a three-day trip to Florence, a lovely little town. It had a famous bridge with shops along both sides of it as part of the bridge. Fortunately, the Japanese didn't destroy the bridge. They just demolished the beginning and the end of it. That way the bridge couldn't be used during the war. As I wandered around the first day there, I discovered a flower show. It was in the open square with little booths all along the side wall. It was not in competition for prizes but to display their wares and hopefully make sales. The next day I returned with my camera to get some photos. Alas! I discovered that it was over and they were cleaning up. On another of my trips I got to Rome and to Pisa. Most visitors to Pisa had their pictures taken with the famous leaning tower. They placed their hand as though they were holding up the tower. In Rome there was much beautiful statuary to be seen. I also got to the Vatican but didn't see the pope.

On my first trip to Rome I bought some seeds in the market. I got sweet peas, zinnias, marigolds, hollyhocks, and phlox. I also got several other kinds of flowers the names of which I didn't recognize in Italian. In addition I bought carrot, watermelon, and honeydew melon seeds. After I got back, one of my tent mates and I planted the seeds. The sweet pea seeds sprouted quickly and started growing nicely. We had planted them along the two sides of the front of the tent. When they began to reach upward, we trained them up some vertical strings fastened to the lower edge of the tent roof. Before long they began blooming, and we were able to pick eight to ten blooms each day.

On my second trip to Rome I did some shopping, even though prices were outrageous. Bookends cost fifteen dollars and twenty cents. A sweater cost thirty dollars. A pair of shoes cost about the same. I bought a Kodak-35 camera and some Kodachrome film for slides. I also met the Italian minister of the Waldensian Church as well as his family. He and his twenty-year-old daughter spoke English. i even had Sunday dinner with them, although I went to the Italian Baptist Church for worship.

In June we had a five-day vacation in Aquila . It is in the midst of beautiful mountains. It had been one of Mussolini's projects for the physical training of Fascist youth. There was an opportunity for horseback riding, which didn't interest me. We were also allowed to go on a few side trips to nearby places of interest.

My most memorable trip was during the Po Valley Campaign. The Italian army personnel were surrendering right and left. I had a three-day break. The Red Cross worker who had introduced me to the cameo shops in Naples invited me to go with her on a trip. We decided to see some of the liberated sites. The only way we were allowed to travel on our own was by hitchhiking. We could only go on an American, British, or French army vehicle. It was easier for us women in uniform to get rides than for the many soldiers.

We had figured on going to Bologna, which was then under the American army jurisdiction. The first lift we got, took us a short distance out of Leghorn. Then we waited just before a bend in the road to try to catch another ride. Before long an American Army jeep came along with only an army captain in it. We hailed him with our thumbs pointing in the direction we wanted to go, but he whizzed on by. However, after a few minutes he returned and picked us up. As we were traveling along, the Red Cross worker asked him where he was going. He answered that he was going to Verona, which was much farther away. She daringly exclaimed that that was where we were wanting to go. Of course, he knew that it could not have been our original plan, but he didn't say anything.

When we were nearly to Verona, we saw an evacuation hospital. We knew that if there was no place yet on bounds in Verona, we could always return to the evacuation hospital. They would take care of us for one night. When we got to the outskirts of Verona, there was an army check post. The sergeant in charge spoke to the captain in whose jeep we were sitting. He said the captain would have to go and talk with the major about us women. He went, and was pleasantly surprised to find that the major was someone he knew. The major asked him what those "fool women" were doing there. The captain replied that we just wanted to see the sights. Well, it turned out that there was one hotel which had just been declared on bounds for army personnel. We could stay there for one night only. Of course, we didn't plan to stay more than one night.

The next morning we started hitchhiking back. The Red Cross worker suggested that we try going back by a different route. We had to make the return trip by a number of short rides. One time we were taken onto a large French army truck that was full of soldiers. They were in the process of trying to spread jelly on slices of bread to eat, and they shared with us. At one point just as I was going to take a bite, the truck hit a bump in the road. With the jolt the slice of bread flew out of my hand onto the road. The soldiers kindly gave me another one.

They left us several miles from Leghorn, but it was already dusk. We wondered if we would have to spend the night there on the road. However, finally an American army vehicle with just two soldiers in it appeared and picked us up. They said that they were going to Leghorn in the morning but would be spending the night in a nearby village. They were sure that the nuns would take care of us also.

It turned out that the two fellows were part of a group that had parachuted in behind the lines. They had then taken over the downstairs of a convent. One of the soldiers was of Italian background and was able to converse with the Italian nuns. They were only too happy to provide meals and other needs to the liberating soldiers. Their unit had moved on to Leghorn. Now these two men had returned for the last load of their supplies and equipment. The nuns had promised them a spaghetti meal. They knew that there would be plenty of food for us also.

While waiting for the food to be finished and dished up, the Red Cross worker tried out their old piano. It was somewhat out of tune, but she was able to play something on it by heart. The nuns were delighted as none of them knew how to play it. The Red Cross worker spoke French and the nuns understood it, so that helped our being accepted. The only kind of music the Red Cross worker knew by heart was jazz. The nuns didn't know the difference and they were thrilled.

After a delicious meal, the nuns said that they would not be allowed to put us women up for the night at the convent. However, they had arranged with one of the women villagers to take care of us. The soldiers took us to the villager's house, and she took us upstairs to where we would sleep. We didn't quite understand what she said on the way up. It sounded as though she said that she had put the priest in the bed for us. We were really startled! It turned out to be a charcoal brazier to warm the bed for us. We had a good night's sleep, and the next morning the two American soldiers got us back to Leghorn. It was the third day of my leave, but the Red Cross worker only had two days off, so she was AWOL. I don't know what penalty she had to pay. I am sure that she thought the adventure was well worth whatever her penalty was.

On June twenty-first I was pleasantly surprised to be promoted to the rank of first lieutenant. Also in June I started studying the Greek New Testament. I had ordered a Beginner's

Greek Grammar and a Greek New Testament from the Baptist Book Store. I found that the first part came to me quickly after the semester of Greek while in college.

The second week of July we were transferred to an evacuation hospital in Leghorn. That meant that we had to leave our garden behind. The sweet peas had been blooming for about three weeks. Also, several other things had just started to bloom, so we got some benefit from it.

They started training us for service in the Pacific Theater, since the war in Europe was over. Among other things we had to learn to use both a carbine gun and a 45 pistol. We learned to dissemble and reassemble them as well as practice shooting at a target. Where we were going we might need to shoot snakes or even enemy soldiers. I am glad that I never had to use a gun in the Pacific Theater. We were told that the Japanese didn't respect the red cross of army hospitals. In fact, they seemed to delight in targeting them.

We also watched a film showing what to do in the event that an enemy soldier started to strangle us with his hands. We should grab his little fingers and pull down, which would keep him from strangling us. Then we should suddenly flip him over our backs. Of course, we didn't actually practice that. I often wondered if I would really be able to flip an enemy soldier over my back like that. However, it was good to be given the idea. At the end of the training we were given a five-day vacation in Stresse on Lake Maggiore. From there we were able to make side trips to Genoa, Milan, and Venice.

I don't remember anything about Genoa, but the cathedral in Milan was beautiful. However, the famous Michael Angelo statue was not there. It had been taken away and hidden somewhere to keep the Japanese from destroying it. Venice was very interesting. The town had no streets at all. All travel was by little boats which went up and down a network of canals. Shops sent their wares around in boats as well. There were boats carrying the types of wares that would interest tourists. There were also boats carrying food and household items for the local villagers.

Soon after our vacation we packed up and got ready to move to the Pacific Theater. Later we learned that we were to go to the Philippines. The morning we were to set sail from Genoa word was received that the Japanese were putting out peace feelers. If the Allies would allow them to keep their emperor, they would surrender. So our orders were changed in case the war should end. Instead of going by way of the Suez Canal, we were to go by way of the Panama Canal. That way, if the war did end, we would already be on our way to the USA. Sure enough, two days later the word was received. The Japanese had surrendered and the war was officially over.

I am an early riser and was up on deck as usual by six a.m. Two days later a voice came over the loud speaker talking in a nonchalant tone of voice. "Perhaps you would like to know that our destination has been changed to Hampton Roads, Virginia." The reaction was electric! Within minutes all the sleepy heads were up on deck. All the sea sick men were cured. Everybody was on deck celebrating! I had never seen them so active, and I couldn't help but laugh to myself .

Of course, we still had to make a zigzag course in order to avoid any torpedo fired from enemy submarines. Thus it still took another two days for us to change course and get to Hampton Roads. When we arrived, the army camp didn't know what to do with us. It was so soon after VJ Day that the army didn't have any orders yet about discharges. For that reason we were allowed to return to our homes for two weeks. Then we were to report to Fort Dix, NJ. Needless to say, my folks were very happy to see me. In the end I was discharged a few days after arriving at Fort Dix.. I had accumulated enough unused leave time to be kept on army salary through the third week of December. Altogether I was in the army for two years and ten months.

# SEMINARY DAYS

Several days after I got home from overseas, the Army decided on the basis for discharge. A notice was published in all of the newspapers that the Army had set up a point system. I figured out that I had enough points to get out of the army. So I thought that now I would have a chance to go to missionary training school. I sent my application to the school in Louisville, KY. I asked if they would accept me even though I would be a few days late.

Two days later I got a long distance phone call from the president of Eastern Baptist Theological Seminary in Philadelphia. He had heard that I expected to be discharged from the army and wanted to get missionary training. He urged me to consider getting my training at the seminary. He wanted me to be their school nurse at the same time. It turned out that my good friend, Mary Asay, from my home church was responsible. She was starting her second year at the seminary. One morning she sat in the dining room at the same table with the house mother. The house mother was lamenting that school had already started but they still didn't have a nurse. If anyone got sick she wouldn't know what to do. Mary's folks had informed her about my plans, so she told the house mother about me.

As soon as the meal was over, the house mother went to the seminary president. She told him about me, and so he called to check with me. I told him that I was tired of my nursing responsibilities keeping me from being active in the local church. He said they could take care of that. He asked me to pray about it. He also suggested that I start my trip to Fort Dix two days early. I could sit in on a few classes and see what the seminary was like before making a decision. That seemed like a good idea, so that is what I did. Soon I had a peace in my heart and mind that this was God's will for me.

Sure enough, I was discharged from the army two days after my arrival at Fort Dix. After I returned to the seminary, I sent a letter to the Missionary Training School in Louisville. I told them that I had changed my mind and decided to get my training elsewhere. God really has a sense of humor. My letter crossed one from there saying that they would be happy to accept me. But they wanted me to be one of their school nurses at the same time!

However, their school was much larger than the seminary. They had two nurses, and it would take me two years to complete one year's study. On the other hand, at Eastern I was the only nurse. Yet I not only took a full course but even a couple of extra courses as well. I only missed a few days because of sick patients. I wore nurses' uniforms the whole two years I was there. That way, students could easily recognize me if they needed me. The doctor came once a week on Wednesdays from eleven a.m. to noon. I could phone him any time if I needed advice or if there was some emergency.

Old Testament Survey, Church History, Biblical Interpretation, and Mission Survey were required subjects in the first semester. In addition I studied voice (singing) and audited Hebrew. I enjoyed all of the subjects except church history. In that course there were so many dates to remember!

The professor of missions, Dr. William Telford, had been a missionary to the Lahu in Burma before the war. He had even translated the New Testament into Lahu. After the war the mission society didn't want to send him back. He was too near retirement age. But working with the Lahu was very much on his heart. In that course he was supposed to teach about the Mission's work in all ten mission fields. When the semester was half over, he suddenly realized that he had only taught us about the work with the Lahu. He hadn't begun to teach us about the work in the rest of Burma nor in the other nine mission fields. His love for the people he had worked with made a deep impression on me.

All of the students were required to have some practical work at one or another of the Baptist churches in the area. Some churches were quite far away, so the students could only go after their Friday classes. Then they could only stay until Sunday evening. In my case because of being the school nurse, I was assigned to the local church. It was just a block away, so I was able to be active in most of the church's activities. I ended up being the Junior Sunday School teacher. Their classes were held in the tower room, but the nearest bathroom was two flights down in the basement.

Exams at the seminary were given just before the Christmas holidays. Then they had to wait two days before the test results came out. Some of the students celebrated the end of exams by going tobaggoning on the snowy slope outside the building. On the very last ride before they planned to quit, they decided to go over a different part of the hill. Unfortunately, they hit a bump somewhere along the way, dropping the tobaggon down about six feet. Three of the students acquired strained backs.

One of the girls, who was mostly skin and bones, got three crushed vertebrae. She was brought back from the hospital in a body cast. The doctors expected she would have to wear it for five to six months.

She soon began walking but sitting down was uncomfortable because she was so skinny. The cast rubbed across her hips. I shared class notes with her for about a week. After that, she began attending classes. She stood at the back of the classroom and rested her notebook on the window sill. Of course, it was my responsibility to take care of her physical needs. Fortunately, after two months the cast was removed and she was given a removable body brace. It was removed when she wanted to lie down, and also when she wanted to have a shower. She could stand up in the shower but I had to wash her.

One Wednesday when the doctor came for his weekly visit, there were no sick patients for him to see. I took advantage of the time to ask him a question I had been wondering about. I still had a bit of occasional pain from the diving accident ten years before. I only had pain the day before my period came, and as soon as my period started the pain disappeared. I was wondering whether I had perhaps caused my uterus to become retroflexed. I told him about the accident and the present symptoms. He replied that he thought I was old enough to have a pelvic exam, which he would like to do. But he would also like to have X-Rays taken of my spine.

These tests revealed that I had crushed my second lumbar vertebra. He explained it like this. Suppose we piled a number of wooden spools one on top of the other. Then suppose we hit them hard with a mallet. One or more of them would split out on the sides as the spools were compressed. That is what had happened to my vertebra. Fortunately, it had not split inwardly so the spinal cord was not injured. Because I was having to give so much care to Ruth with her crushed vertabrae, this really impressed me.

Betty Clarke, my prayer mate from seminary and nurses' training days, was discharged from the army several months after I was. She decided to attend the missionary training course at Eastern beginning with the second semester. However, no more beds were available for her, so I ended up having a roommate. It certainly was good to see her and to be able to have prayer sessions with her again. She took all but two of the courses I was taking, so we were together much of the time.

In the second semester we had more courses than in the first. However, some of them were for just one hour a time, instead of two. The two-hour course was New Testament Survey. The one-hour courses were Principles of Christian Education, Child Education, Evangelism, and Pastor's Assistant. The two courses Betty couldn't take were the continuation of Mission Survey and of Biblical Interpretation. I also took New Testament Greek and piano. She also took organ lessons

I spent most of the Easter vacation typing Mary Asay's thesis. The next week I finished a term paper of my own. I also typed two and a half other term papers for classmates, getting paid for the latter. The week after that I finally completed reports on one thousand pages of collateral reading. Final exams were held in mid-May and the semester ended on the thirty-first of May.

I returned home on Saturday, June first, and remained there for one week before going to Romney, New Hampshire. I was at Romney for two weeks of training sponsored by the

New England Fellowship. The purpose was so that we could do Vacation Bible Schools (VBS) in churches in New England through the end of July. The training was held at the conference grounds in the White Mountains and was beautiful. Sunday was for worship and free time. Beginning the next day classes were held morning, afternoon, and evening. Then we were divided into teams of two or three each to hold VBS in the various churches.

Our team was composed of two girls and one boy. We were first sent to Rockland, ME. The people were very friendly, and the church was quite spiritual. The Vacation Bible School seemed to be quite a success also. We had more than one hundred the first week. Then it dropped to about ninety the second week because some of the children developed measles. Fourteen juniors and four primaries gave their hearts to the Lord. Our closing night program was a success. The offering came to $77.65, which was divided between the three of us.

Only us two girls were sent on to a small New England town, Brooklyn. It was on the Atlantic coast with a small two-room church. The situation there was almost the opposite from the previous one. They had not had a pastor since February, though they had been trying out various candidates. Apparently there were five or six church members who were fundamental believers. The rest were evidently quite liberal and definitely not spiritual.

We were put in a house reserved for summer people, and we ate breakfast there. Most of the other meals were eaten at different homes in the community. The church had done nothing to prepare for the Vacation Bible School. We arrived to find no advertising, no helpers, no plans of any sort. In fact, no provision had been made for our needs. One of the fundamentals had studied in a Bible School in Providence, RI, for one semester. Finally, he took upon himself to arrange for our first few meals, and to transport us. He even took us around the town Sunday afternoon to the homes where there were children. That enabled us to invite them to our VBS. We were finally able to persuade one woman to help us by taking charge of the preschool children. However, she had to bring along her three-year-old daughter in order to do so.

We two girls prayed together often as we faced one problem after another. The Lord helped us and enabled most things to work out to His glory. We had fourteen children the first day, twelve the next day in spite of heavy rain, and seventeen the third day. We didn't try to have it on the fourth day because it was a holiday. The attendance continued about the same for the remainder of the two weeks.

On Wednesday of the second week the woman who was teaching the preschool class had a complaint. She told me that at recess time she had left her purse on the table and went out with the children. When she returned, her purse was gone. She suspected one little girl who didn't participate in the playing. She figured that the girl might have slipped back into the room and taken the purse.

When the mother of the child came to get her child at noon, I spoke to her. I asked her that if she saw her child with money she shouldn't have to please let me know. Immediately, she was angry, saying her child was not a thief. If we were going to accuse her falsely like that, she wouldn't bring her child any more. Sure enough, the child didn't return again.

That afternoon the one who thought her purse had been stolen phoned me and apologized. She said that when she returned home, she found her purse on the table. She was a little late and had failed to take it with her. I went to the woman who had been offended and apologized. However, she remained offended at the woman who had been teaching the children. Otherwise, the closing program was a success. I returned home and spent the whole month of August there, glad to be with Daddy and my brother and my home church friends again.

Four happenings in particular stand out in my memory concerning my second year of seminary. The first one had to do with my prayer mate, Betty Clarke. It seemed that a fellow classmate Addison Truxton, had a brother who worked for Missionary Aviation Fellowship (MAF). He came to visit his Addison. In the dining room when he saw Betty, he asked his brother to introduce him to her. Then he told her that as soon as he saw her, he immediately felt assurance in his heart that she was the one he was to marry. Naturally she was amazed. However, we had already been praying about her desire to find a husband if that were God's plan for her. Still she didn't want to make a mistake by being hasty. We kept on praying about it and he kept in touch with her. By the time she graduated, she was sure that it was right. So they got married the next day. They had many blessed years of marriage until her death in February 2012.

The second happening had to do with my research paper. We were given the choice of either writing a thesis or doing a research paper. I preferred the latter. However, I wanted to do research on some matter that would really be helpful to some organization. I wrote to the American Baptists as well as to the Southern Baptists. The Southern Baptists said that they were planning to start a new work in Argentina in the near future. They needed to know what other mission agencies were already working there. They also wanted to know what those organizations were doing and where. So that's the project I chose to research. The information I was able to find for them was a real help, they said. Using the data I had provided helped them decide where in Argentina to start their new work.

The third happening had to do with Missions Day. Once a year the seminary gave a day to a special missions emphasis. The purpose was to challenge the students to consider going into missionary work following graduation. My first year there the program was very disappointing to me and my classmates. I began talking with each of my classmates in turn getting their suggestions. We were trying to think of what could be done the following year to make the program more meaningful.

Several months before Missions Day in the second year, I took the suggestions I had to the staff person in charge and consulted with her. She was pleased with the suggestions and asked me and my classmates to take charge. I no longer remember details as to what we did. But I do know that the Lord blessed us with a highly informative and inspirational program.

The fourth happening started two months before graduation. One of my classmates, Grace Turley, asked me what I planned to do after I graduated. I replied that I believed God wanted me to be a foreign missionary. But I didn't know yet where He wanted me to go. She said, "Emilie, what's wrong with us? It's only two months before we graduate. Yet not a single member of our class knows exactly what the Lord wants him or her to do."

Well, that got me to thinking. I could hear a missionary tell about his/her work in Africa and it would interest me. I would think, "I'd love to do that if that was what God wanted for me." Then the next day I could hear a missionary tell about the work in China. Again I would think, "I'd love to do that if that was what God wanted me to do." But how was I expecting to discover what God wanted *me* to do?

So, I began to pray and to study the New Testament to seek guidance. The passage that helped me the most was Acts 16:6-10. Paul and his companions tried to go to Asia but the Spirit hindered them. Then they tried to go to Bithynia and again the Spirit hindered them. But they didn't just sit there and wait for God's leading. Rather, when God closed a door here, they looked for where there was an open door. They went that way until God stopped them. Again they looked for an open door and ended up in Troas. There the vision of the man from Macedonia made sense to them.

Once I saw this, I made a pledge to the Lord. From that moment on, if I saw anything that looked like an open door, I would enter it. I would then trust the Lord to close a door here and open a door there until He led me to where He wanted me to go.

Two days later at the end of a missions class my professor asked me what I planned to do after graduation. I answered as usual that I believed God wanted me to become a foreign missionary but I didn't know yet where He wanted me to go. He then asked me what kind of missionary work I wanted to do. I explained that I envisioned myself as working with a backward people. I saw them as illiterate, not knowing how to keep healthy, and not knowing the Lord. He replied, "There's just the place for you with my Lahu people in northeast Burma."

Having made the pledge to the Lord, I asked him what I should do. He said, "*It just happens* that two days from now the candidate secretary from the American Baptist Foreign Missionary Society will be speaking in chapel. Afterwards, he will hold conferences with any students interested in becoming a missionary. So you go and have a conference with him and he will tell you what to do" That's what I did. I was given a two-page form to fill out. It would establish communication with the mission board. Yet it wouldn't commit either me or them to anything final.

Before long I received a response from the mission board. They said that they had already appointed a couple to work with the Lahu. They felt that they could not appoint someone else to work with the Lahu until some of the other needs were met first. Seeing that I was a nurse, they wondered if I would consider working in a mission hospital. Three mission hospitals badly needed more missionary nurses. One was in China and two were in India. I replied that I really believed that I could do a better job in a village situation than in a hospital. Yet I didn't dare tell the Lord what I would or would not do. If they knew that and still felt that a hospital was where I was needed the most, I would go. I would then do the best I could.

I was sent a four-page form to fill out, asking me to go and work in a mission hospital in Northeast India. The morning that I was going to put the form into the mail, I got another letter from the mission board. In it they said that they had changed their minds. Hazel Shank, the Board representative for Burma and India, was visiting those two countries. They wanted to wait until her return and let her make the final decision. I went ahead and sent the filled-out form as it was, but I enclosed a letter. In it I said, "You asked me to consider going to the hospital in Northeast India, so I thought that must be God's will for me. But perhaps He was just testing me to see if I would really be willing to go anywhere. At any rate, I'll be praying for God to guide you in your decision."

Among my fellow students at seminary were Paul and Elaine Lewis. Paul told me that he and his wife planned to attend the Summer Institute of Linguistics in Norman, OK, during the summer. I decided that I would like to do so also. It consisted of nine weeks of the methods of putting a language into writing. This was followed by a two-week period of practice.

Teams of six students were assigned to one American Indian informant. The informant knew English, but was not allowed to use it with us. Each of the team members had one hour in which to ask the informant how they say various things. For example, one might say, "How do you say 'I eat'?" Then, "How do you say, 'You eat,'?", etc. Whatever was different in the two sentences was obviously the way that the pronouns were expressed. All six of us could take notes on what was said. But only the one whose turn it was could talk with the informant. Every couple of days we had a session with a staff member. There we shared what we understood at that point and what questions we had. The results of our discussions served as the basis for questioning the informant in the remaining sessions. At the end we each wrote up in proper linguistic format an analysis of as much of the language as we had learned

A Karen from Burma named McCarthy Gyaw was studying at the University of Oklahoma there in Norman. When Paul learned about him, he and his wife got permission use him as their informant. They wanted to analyze the Burmese language instead of working on one of the Indian languages. Then I got permission to use him as my informant also and analyze his Karen language. I didn't know at that point that I would end up working with Karens, but the Lord knew and led me in this decision. However, I opted to also audit an Indian language as part of a team. That way I could learn from the guidance of the staff member.

Our team's informant was a Comanche Indian woman. I worked with the others but didn't write up that language. I only wrote up the Karen language. Having an aptitude for languages, I really enjoyed this course. In fact, I caught on so quickly that I also got permission to sit in on several second-year classes as well. One of the leaders in the Summer Institute of Linguistics was Dr. Eugene Nida. Some years later he told me that he had written to the American Baptist Mission Board and urged them to appoint me as a missionary. He told them that my facility in learning languages would help me become an effective missionary.

Soon after Hazel Shank got back from her trip to Burma and India, she sent for me. She asked me to tell her why I didn't want to work in a hospital. I explained about my hospital experiences which had resulted in my having an inferiority complex when in ward work. Also, it was my understanding that missionary nurses mostly did supervision and teaching. What I liked was the contact with the patients.

Then she asked me how I would like to work with the Karen people of Burma. At that time I knew practically nothing about them. Of course, I already had some idea of the structure of the language. When she told me about them I realized that their situation was just what I had wanted. There was an exception to what I had envisioned. A few of their leaders had studied abroad and come back as physicians or seminary professors. Some of them were already well educated having trained in their own country. However, many in the villages were illiterate and knew little about good health practices or about Jesus Christ. Immediately I had peace in my heart and mind that this was God's plan for me.